As Her Eyez Kiss

Tari Sai,
Blessing to the souls
of a relaxed night.
wish the innocense of love
through poetic verse touches you

26 Apr 07

Cover designed by: Gabrielle Smith @ www.gabriielle.com
Edited by: Roberta Boyd
Copyright © 2006 Mervyn R. Seivwright
All rights reserved.
"All right reserved including the right of reproduction in whole or in part in any form"

Printed by: Booksurge Publishing
ISBN: 1-4196-4644-3

Manufactured in the United States of America
For contact with author go to
http://www.MervynSeivwright.com
Available also on the web site is Mervyn Seivwright's
First two books "Trials Of A Stranger", "Through Their Eyez"
And his audio poetry CDs "Shedding My Skin" and "Breathe"
Email: deepcobra@MervynSeivwright.com

To order additional copies, please contact us.
BookSurge, LLC
www.booksurge.com
1-866-308-6235
orders@booksurge.com

As Her Eyez Kiss
Poems

Mervyn R. Seivwright

2006

As Her Eyez Kiss

As Her Eyez Kiss

As her eyez kissed mine
I loved her before the word love ever thought to come to
    my lips.
Large brown eyez deep seated into each part of my
    existence.
Every molecule I had gravitated to her.
As I was as her,
was of her,
was one with her,
with each breath
I look to duplicate internally never knowing externally to
    feel the love she bore to me.
I have met shes that were from city streets,
to them that are country sweet,
across to the ones who were taught to be classy.
From them very appealing to the eyez,
to those appealing to make my warm vibrate senses
    happy.
Never quite able to emulate that first love.
Seeking to complete that first unconditional deep
    spiritual love

While seeking I have kissed eyez in regions of at least four
    of the seven seas
Eyez that picture shes
that are laced into the word expressions that I present but
    not define

Definition not explained by the first look,
fragment of their time that I took,
the mental daily food shared that they cook
not defined as the black ink layered on the pages of a book

So I edify those that make up the chemistry of my energy.
How they embraced me with dimensions richer than a
    physical touch
I birth these thoughts to celebrate
how much life's interaction of these shes meant to me.
Some were just images of time seen,
friends I carry to eternity,
individual spirits that I met just to connect at certain spots
    of my timeline
or a possible soul mate like perfecting wine ingredients to
    age
before flavor blends with the tongue

I am just blessed to have been among figurines of angelic
    wonder
from beyond cirrus clouds
Beyond those clouds I see
gold hues rise twisting into early morning skies
    remembering…
Just remembering…
as her eyez kissed.

**Imagery of Her
(Igbo)**

Ofu

These words are to simply admire
Not to pursue or desire your spirit or in the flesh
I am trying to capture your internal essence that came so
   well dressed
Essence that has walked this earth seven times

She, was priestess to Isis in ancient Kemet
Closet to Isis glory, the nubia that young daughters seek
Ra desired to drink her spirit,
More wondrous than the blossom of the skies that he
   reaped

Her eyes were remembered in Mali,
centuries before western civilization pillaged the land.
The daughter of a king who rose in Africa,
and warriors fought,
to show their bravery and seek her will.

I heard of her voice in Timbuktu, the only teacher that
   was known, as not man.
Griots tell stories of her lessons of family,
the reason why for 400 years this empire did stand.

She was like a ghost to the Moorish clan.
Her spirit was the wind that whistled direction in their
 travels throughout the European land.
She… worshipped in dreams, a vapor that nature tapered
 to bring Spanish men to their knees.

They spoke of her as the youngest daughter of Shaka,
fighting spirit as her father,
Charismatic in her thunder to lead men.
Her ambiance commanded obedience in the hearts of
 those Zulu men.

Songs of her rise in festival dance cries deep in the
 mountains of Palmeres
She is the muse in which warriors float by, as the graceful
 movements of Caparia
That sting and slide, escape and glide in for
 unconventional attacks,
but not lacking victory.
Her muse has never died since their history.

Last night, the ancestors spoke to me through the stars.
Mentioned of your silence to walk with the common
 man,
Though still possessing your glory.
Your smile, not losing its light since the Egyptian sun.
Your voice, still sings with spirit that brought life to the
 Palmerian ones.

Your stature, its Zulu power, one that men still venture
 to see.
You are the spirit and image of a multidimensional screen.
Just a blessing from the angels to walk in man's twilight.
I am blessed, in a fragment, just to catch sight of her.

Abua

Presence of angelic waterfalls lay a mist before me
As I peer upon an image that seems beyond
    comprehension
She appeared from sunset raindrops
Or the Andes Mountains descending off the cloud tops
Royalty honored with starry delight, and the warmth of
    the sun's embrace
Though she is in the presence of commoners
So I must tread softly for her majestic wonder
Knowing she must, of blessed boardwalks and fashion
    talks
Of heavenly skies
Tears cry of her beauty…
Bathed in creams and essences of the 7 seas
Skin moisture and touch purr of compressed rose petals
Eyes grip souls as emeralds of lost worlds
From a lost time…
Time of Egyptian stories…
Stories of a Princess of the Nile, that commoners adored
She is the missing daughter of Isis
And passionately pursued as a whisper by Ra
The Eye of the Pyramid that sparked desert shadows
This presence that I see in crystallized appearance upon
    my eyes
How could it be that this exotic flower and this locale is
    laced
I know at this time, and environment
    she is out of place.

Ato

Those milk cocoa colored eyes
Those deep moving, rich, heart touching eyes
Plague my mind like drug highs
Desiring to know your deepest secrets
What elevates that smile?
Like the silver lining of the clouds in the sky
I feel your glowing presence before I see
Birds like Larks in spring
Is what I hear when your voice does sing
Questions in my mind what can complete you
Your inner passion,
sense of fashion,
the pride in what you do
My impression of you will forever last
You for me, not a lifetime task
Just to respect the dwelling beauty
From internal to outside shell
Dreams that venture through my mind
To pray I grow gray enough to tell
The feeling that those eyes that intertwined my mind
Of visions so free
These images so special,
Of this deep chocolate queen

Anô

She sung with the birds that echoed heaven's chimes
Feeling the resonance start before the sound grew to
    vibrate in me
Then I saw her angelic milk chocolate face.
Laced with the elements from ancestors in kingdoms
    once before.
Storytellers that grew thirsty on the essence she
    possessed.
She, named from joined phrases of the skies,
seas, and earth from the time of her birth.
Knowing they searched the stars seven times before they
    uttered her name.
Seven, the number of perfection from the first glance of
    her eyes.
Eyes that hypnotized the mind of voice imagery
as a siren bringing sailors to find their depth
in oceans that swept across the earth's unlinked
    patchwork.
Her spirit danced as spring;
Birth of the colors new life sings
in waves
on beached shores
as light brought the cold darkened winters.
She was the light
where only darkness could be found.
Her voice electrified streetlights
that guided my path before I saw her.
She that has seen the pains & cries

of her people though a symbol of hope
as long as she is able to rock lullabies to those that seek
    evil.
She is the silent queen that shares her spirit
without royalty reflecting the jewels of her crown that
    blare from inside.
Inside, I hear heaven's chimes
…in her whispers

Ise

Smooth caramel
textured skin upon her face
Not able to see
the destination of the face
No smile or sigh
dictating expression
Name of French descent
laced on her dress
In her symbol of the free,
and home of the brave
On this world she claims
Sunrays glare on her aura
through small gaps of window tint
Showing the inner
light she possesses
Hair, a reddish-charcoal,
sleek back to look uniform
Opening up the warmth of her soul
A Pandora's box
an unknown to unfold
While peering at the smooth
caramel textured skin upon her face.

Isii

I have found morning
Morning like the springtime's first day
A rebirth of life has drawn upon my soul as I pray.

I have found morning
Fresh dew drop have awakened my eyes
My vision is of a soft mocha
A precious mocha, one that as this princess shall rise

I have found morning
Face is full with the light of day
Eyes like stars that lead your lit pathway
Gentle & sleek like silk to touch
If I am dreaming, never wake me, so I may continue to lay

I have found morning
Voice of a new bird's morning call
Like a lark, its vibrations stalk my soul
Singing a song of peace unto me
Is this the key to set my inner mind free?

I now see morning
I pray to my Lord for guidance first today

And praise for the shared true inspiration blessing me this new day
Fresh breath of this morning fills my lungs
Eyes wide remembering each second as night is now done

Asaa

Petals velveteen soft and smooth caramel
sapphire eyes shining of gold
orchid so precious
a delicate glory
her smile glows like sunshine
no darkness can come to thee
hair dark like coal
like the mane of a stallion
smells of the scent which the orchid possesses
tropical flower and symbol she bonita
not a flaw I can question
a lady
a queen
these words are the picture
I'll always remember
Kodak, the picture brings this image to life
you are the picture of this inspiration
words to touch you this time in your life

Asato

I try to patiently find the words to define
the rich deepness of the soul in your presence I see.
A sistah full of character
the world has not sought the truth in thee.
Beauty enhancing from within that inspires the outside
    shell.
Chocolate, pure extraordinary
inner passion
do you seek to know her well.
Her desire for strength is the drive to fuel her day by day.
This strength is in triple fold,
that is what I see displayed.
Mental strength your daily task,
a night and daytime tale.
Day is the deep mental personal interactions,
night is the knowledge to rise you higher
building a solid foundation never to fail.
Spiritual strength your inner power to discern things you
    are told,
knowing He who guides you,
a light that will not let your fire grow cold.
Physical strength like iron,
newly formed from the firing well.
Never cold,
body form is smooth but bold,
an appearance that is not frail.
A Nubian Queen,
looks of royalty flow through her cheeks and smile.

Her blood boils golden essence like the gently guided
    Nile.
These few words have embraced my mind
to reach beyond your eyes and ears.
To reconfirm the image you give,
like a drug I inhale your vibe so clear.

Iterani

Shimmering in the breeze
Off sunlight passes clear texture
Wings of external, an awe to see
A thing of beauty before thee
Flying in my mind this precious kind
Of the Lord's natural blessing to the world

Eyes of crystal sparkle & shine
Deep within the soul intertwined
Examining self worth to find
If your mentals are as a rose does flourish

These are simple words of perception
Not for misleading thoughts of direction
Looking into this vision I see
Her, this crystal butterfly before me.

Ili

Miles tell me about her
As your jazz vibe penetrates my mind
Feeling her vibrations in me,
A spirit internally roaming free
It is known to her already who I am
And knowing that she is that ideal woman
Your strong spirit leaves me in awe
Presence from you, I have not felt before
True in nature, down to the inner core
Already my heart, in you, I adore
Mind elevation, to feel your sensations
Feel the deep penetration of your soul
You are that ideal woman
Woman, with joy and laughter
Quick feet to dance the night until after
A head to cry on
In my words like a new song
Listening to your lyrical voice
A lark singing smoothly like a river at race
An ideal woman of choice
Dreaming thoughts of a future,
praying to this, I wish to embrace
Understanding that tomorrow is filled with His vision
So today, stands this man, with no demands
Just desiring to feel you
The true you, that most don't ever get through to

You, molded and shaped from God's glory
The one African Queen deeply rich story
As I feel the vibrato of Miles's horn blow as inside it can
Yes, I know you would be my ideal woman

Ili na ofu

Eyes as bright
and blue
as the sky's clearest day
Clear, piercing
deeply felt inside
Soft flaming hair
floating in the wind
My eyes never leave her
Eyes magnetic to her
Only wishing
to remember her face
Adoring her face
And the soul
beneath the face
Every time I see
My eyes desire to embrace thee
The butterfly before me.

Ili na abua

Autumn pigments welcome the flight of the Russian
    butterfly
I sense its vibrant scents and beautiful appeal
So slender, but not so frail
A rare sight of God's blessings, from its' balance,
I can tell
I feel the power of the wings
Your vibes felt through your mental wonders
Wings rushing wind into my lungs
To drive me full of life and splendor
I watch you
Watch you closely
Almost like a busy bee darting to and fro
Feeling you as if you are to become the root of my spine
Deeply feeling your presence
I open to you, my nectar
Nectar of a soul that has fermented over time
Waiting to see if one could find
Find that only a true butterfly can blossom
I am the destination of the compass stitched on your skin
Waiting for the moment of conception of a blended life to
    begin
Waiting...
Waiting...
On this Russian Butterfly I wait
With a yearning, passionate burning moment
to truly seek your soul.

Dreams of Her
(Mandinka)

Kiling

She was sunshine,
You know the kind on the outskirts of Nairobi,
Sistah queen on the plains where the land meets the sky.
Her high cheeks secured her warm smile
Smile that vibrated my skin bumps
Chills that increased my heart beat thump
Memories echoed from that cinco de septembre, day in
    fall or autumn
As some call it…
She was as an autumn rainbow, leaves with colours from
    sand to ebony,
Laced together to dress her skin.
Remember I saw the sundress against her skin.
Though I searched high & low to find.
What would best provide her essence?
Feeling I would have to teach myself
to stitch thread by thread to design what would reflect
    her royal presence.
Her innocent face, embraced my mind,
But knowing her spirit wouldn't seek mine.
Though she floats like vapors in ghost form that has now
    just blown away.
When I held her I closed my eyes and focused on her
    heart inside
Feeling soft beats stimulate the patterns of my mind.
Last night she blessed my mental easel
For my dreams painted each stroke that her beauty did
    provide

This morning I gasp my first breath
It was her I must attest,
I have breathed her since our last farewell as I held her
    close to me

Fúla

Silence is a silent face
What are the words when our eyes embrace?
It seems like our souls in time were to meet
Though verbal silence will come to defeat
This is what I sense from my heart about you
A women of class, frail and sensitive too
Beauty from within,
that glorifies through
As I put my head down,
I pray Lord what should I do
Fill me with wisdom,
in heart and in mind
Give me the knowledge
so I can provide
The words so sincere,
for the lady before me
Her presence an aura
that I cannot describe to thee
It makes me feel strangely,
it's good without answer
Pour out your essence,
in my hand at this time
For it is so precious
for deep understanding
So I won't seek darkness,
but in your heart,
a light I'll find

To lead me onward in the right direction
Then you can receive my honest affection
A man of sensitivity you will find
Behind the words
in my quiet mind.

Sàba

I am yearning you
Long dreams
and waking up from cold sweats
bubbling on my skin.
I pain within
Waiting for that day
wishing it was yesterday
Having memories of us
A comfort unsurpassed,
No space
between our passionate grasp
Searching every part of you
is my task
Tears fall from my heart
A beating only desiring
to beat when I am close to you
Soft rub down of your skin
I wish to feel, knowing that you
are truly real
Not these sleepless nights
which only you could heal
I yearn each second
to touch your mind
What inner mental depth
can I reach and find
For my internal soul
is yours to climb

Scenes of you in the rain,
on the beach,
white crest waves
I wish to touch you
now as I yearn
Yearn...
Yearn looking that you are my
Yesterday
Today,
and Tomorrow

Naani

If we were nearer our hearts would be much dearer
If we weren't committed, deep love we could have submitted
If we were single, would our minds had even mingled
If we let the lines go, would the embracement of our minds just explode
If we had a first kiss, would our partners we miss
If we physically embraced, could just a friendship be retraced
If we stop contact now, would the pain be profound
If we continue like this, your full trinity I would wish
If we feel reality's card dealt, why is this confusion in my mind felt?
If, this word of non-absolution, drawing no conclusion to what is or what is to be
All I know is in one lifetime I let my mind and heart roam free
Or a prison, I place myself in mentally
Absolution is communication isolation flow
You and I knowing exactly what our feelings know
But because of the IF variable we'll never know
Unless the IFs you just let go
IF...
IF...

Luulu

I see her
Yes I see her
Her is that she
That possesses the world I see
She is that voice
Speaking in the wind
Swishing in the trees
Blowing in morning calls
A blessing on me
I pray does fall
I feel her
Her presence that seeks
Felt through vibes
That brings warmth to my soul
Yes, she that embraces me
Completes the existence that could have
Should have
Would have
Have…
I currently have not
Not she…her…
The one blessed from above
I hear her
Her speaking to me
Words…
Words…that echo through my mind
Drowning out the words defined

My sense of focus I cannot find
My heart has ceased to live
So dies
I see her
Her is that she
That she inside me
Wishing to just be
Ghost....

Wooro

Days are passing
since our inceptions,
as water waves flow
within our bodies
controlled by celestial shifts,
thoughts of you
are a constant calm that drift endlessly.
Never going without spirit of you
since you blended
into my mental anatomy.
Dreams of You

Worowula

Like smelling wine
The vapors succumb before my face
The flavor yet to know, feels...
No bottle that I can embrace
But these vapors like protruding dreams that are giving
 endless thoughts
The smell is rich, with possessive charm
Could it cause some mental harm?
A quiet desire to feel a liquid saturation
While I am spending endless days in a desert formed
 dehydration
Is the age I feel a good year?
Is the flavor sweet or dry?
Is it a blush that's mixed with sweetness & spirit strong
 possessed?
Once I can enjoy the flavor I can put these thoughts to
 rest
To enjoy good wine takes an endless time
A long term, patience thing
As these vapors rise
To bring my mind these highs
From this scent that these vapors bring

Sayi

You wish to know my dreams of you
Dreams like desires,
These words must be thought through
As I journey across a dangerous path
I feel fuzzy, knotted up,
Not a smile,
Not a laugh
Endless dreams, day and night pour into my head
Scenes of her imagery turn like pages being read
I wish to massage you
Your body and mind
To share your total balance,
you took a lifetime to find
Please teach me to reach inside
And make it pour out to you
Feel my tight but soft skin embrace
Let me feel your mind too
Show me deep inspiration
That you have filled deep in me
Show me visions of expressions
All you want me to see
Let me hold you in passion
Through your eyes pure as pearls
Your lyrical voice makes me tremble
Like a God sent blessed bird
I can see you with a smile
Within depths of your face

I pray that you let me give you joy
Not disgrace
I have crossed many lines
With these words sincere and true
But I am sorry...
My dreams see me
In the comfort of you.

Kònonto

Oh sistah,
such a vision you place before me.
As I hide behind my conformed society garments
that represent a false sense of peace.
My eyes have gazed upon you many a days
In daydream wonder at your coffee chocolate,
soft, smooth porcelain textured skin
Lips so full & rich with the appearance of embroidered
    silk.
Cheeks firm, but of cotton soft to touch
Curves, that swirl the world,
like Italian crystal precious as pearls
Physical transition to the mental
Creativity that blossoms
like the 'Bird of Prey', from the islands.
Heart of a lioness when on the prowl,
Strong & passionate the mind flows as the vision shows
So my desire to write does grow
My thoughts are expressions to touch your mind
Before you leave & are hard to find
Expectations to let you feel the images I see
Not a desire from,
but to uplift you…
This woman…
An African Queen

Vibes of Her
(Yoruba)

Okan

My writing stumbled as I heard her
She lost in yesterday's future
She the likes of Bessie, Ella, or Nina
She poured deep into the blues of today's yesterday
Today we don't feel yesterday
Don't feel the spirit of yesterday flow in us.
She had me looking back at my life since birth to my first
    love
My first love…
I remember looking at her
Eyes tearing of joy from our embrace
Barely able to focus my eyes on her
But I loved her
My mother's eyes staring at me…
Hearing her song to seek the comfort of my sleep
Hearing her brought me back to her Congo.

Eji

Before I saw her mouth open…
Each hair on my skin was on edge,
vibrating to her early dawn bird song
Song that reminded me of the power of music
Her music could soothe the most savage of beasts
Her voice could bring warring factions to peace
Her voice is the melody of the mountain winds to the
    deep valley streams.
Her voice let me live stories & dreams

I have heard her
But don't hear her like I feel her
I feel her articulate my blood stream to pulsate
Synchronizing my heart to her voice vibrate
She must have passed spirits with either the muse
of Curtis Mayfield or Billie Holiday
Knowing her stories will move generations
She will move the lost and the found
Those in shallow waters & profound
From them seeking hope,
And those with deep spiritual beliefs
Bring health to the sick,
Bring life to those a second from death

Her spirit regenerates internally for each second to re-live my first breath
She brings my soul to physical form to just taste her harmony
To leave my own inner existence to fly free,
On the resonance of the vapors that now cloud my mind
Clouds me with clairvoyance to see through the hearts of men
Imagery of music that tells their stories
Or leads them,
to seek themselves,
about the wealth that internally they may not possess

Her voice must have led choirs of angels
For her angelic voice conducts the bird's morning call in a dreaming harmony
I believe her vibrations have dwelled in my history
Since the second from the baby crib to bring me to peace
She has echoed within my heart's chambers
So even if I was deaf in life
I would have lived to her melody
I wonder if they can hear her in the breeze
And be blessed by the she in thee

Meta

Eternal soft breeze
Bleeds feverishly in me
Eyes reached internal
Old soundless film memories
The harmonic voice
Chimed in my heart hypnotically
A blossomed spirit
Orchids came from within thee
Aphrodite's charm
God's breathless speechless beauty
Eternal touched me angelically

Merin

Song Bird... I feel the tone of your harmony
Glisten its vibrato
Vibrating tones to calm my soul
My whole... Inside
Melodies whispering the singing of a siren
Reaching out to me completely
Hearing your voice I felt you
Like the wind rushing through the meadows
Deep green pastures...
where wild flowers grow
Penetrating my skin down to my toes
Bright sun warms my outer clothes
You bring me wonders like snow capped mountains
As far as the vision of my eyes can go
For this inside I know
You are the mystery...
That I have questioned
To me a blessing...
Passionate soul I know you share
I know when I do see you
Question if I could complete you
You share the aura I possess
Your vision brings me inner strength
Your beauty internal to outside is heaven sent
As I wait, your songs of words will keep me
Bring my blood to life to feel free
Yes, your inspiration
Is truly my inner key

Marun

Pouring internally like 100 feet cliffs
Black liquid crystals sparkle the lights of your spirit
As our eyes kiss...
I feel your joys, pain and the effervescence of your
　　essence
I feel your soul drain on me
I feel your soul enlighten me
I feel your soul as a ghost possess me
Looking deep into your blacq pearl eyes
Pearls full of richness priceless in the heavens
Your pearls shimmer as mountain streams briskly
Shape your everlasting beauty.
Shimmer as ocean waves
lighting up the midnight darkened moonlit sky
Your spirit shivers my skin hairs to stand on edge
Waving in the wind like mid-west wheat fields
You are the image on canvas that I wouldn't sell for a
　　lifetime
I would bury it with I until my last breath
So that your soul will seek after mine
Never holding you physically with me
I still feel your essence as raindrops fall on me for an
　　eternity
Never needing to embrace your lips, your skin, or your
　　presence
I am filled with your aura
since each glance has set me free.

Mefa

Lucky which way the wind will turn
Bend, twist, twirl, wiggle, unnatural in its natural form.
It knows its path in life, but unpredictable to all it
    impresses upon
It brings shine & storms, and confusion across lands &
    waters
Can you feel the rain coming?
I see the rain determined & strong
Art work in the making, the world it is taking
The rain can spawn dreams of a lifetime
With the pitter-patter of the hypnotic raindrop beat
Leaving the soul blind
Like a mental demonstration
What is the total persuasion?
It is the silky dreams caused by the steady pounding
Of a rhythmic sound to my sweet slumber
The misery from an endless seemed eternity with
    lightning & thunder
Putting joy under in its cold painful twist
Maybe the passion from a spell in the springtime
Happens from heat beaded drops upon my limbs that are
    bare
Does the rain even care?
But motivated by the wind
Will you, the wind, ever tell me how you blow?
So maybe I will know
What kind of rain may soak my name?
Penetrating these thoughts to endure

Meja

This morning, I could smell you coming through my
    windows
Tropical winds of glory brought your essence to me
I could see your color in the tropical flowers outside
Seeing your beauty
… …
I paused and thought of you…
Yes an internal poetic bliss of you comforting me
Surrounding me…
You are the mist in the new summertime
As I look up to the white cotton clouds
The air possesses your spirit that I find…
From this morning upon first breath you have been on my
    mind

Mejo

You are the dawn
that gives early warmth to the day
Sharing your light
glared from the aura you display
Feeding the first meal to nature's hunger
Letting it peer onward to the world in beauty
You are the vapors
energizing each molecule of life to breathe
Breathing in me…
Seeing your daily blessings upon me
I see your rays develop the awesome wonders
expressed from what you reflect
You are the piercing fire
that internally moves me onward
Missing your glowing spirit
as the absence of your presence each night in me departs
Since you're the sun rays…
glowing for an eternity…
to the world and internally
Sunrays for your beauty and entirety
a blessing in which I daily see

Mesan

Internally, externally
A balance I'll define
A concept many times requested
Though very hard to find

Beauty is the concept spoken
Beauty is where the balance lies
Beauty is in the eyes of one
But the depth is the bottom line

External beauty, a youthful thing
That battles the eves of time
But easily does change its look
From ugliness inside

Internal beauty, like ivy
Overgrows the outside shell
But take care of the outer
Or the inside you will never see to tell

Balance is the factor
Where true beauty is found

You must have inner confidence
But too much is profound

Humbleness in theory
And self-external preservation is the guide
Now ask yourself the question
What is in you?
Is it true beauty that you find?

Mewa

Seconds are like hours feeling cold
urges remembering each yesterday
Remembering your voice, face,
and the touch of your tender hands.
Your warmth is like summer fields of purple, and gold
    wild flowers
On the lower plateaus of the mountains of this land.
Rich green grass and you in a summer dress
bring more life to the valley.
Picnic for 2,
I see you there,
a bottle of white wine and sandwiches to share.
Blanket laid out so we can feel the sun, birds singing
    lyrical songs,
breeze whistling on our skin, but warm.
Feeling your eyes kiss.
Kissing vibe easing through my spine,
glowing my spirit.
Your voice is like the lark
giving harmonies inspiring movements of calmness and
    comfort.
Being in your comfort feeling your vibe.
Vibes I was blessed with from a higher power.
Vibes that are the aura from your inner presence.
Vibes that fill my mind with my intellectual find.
Vibes of your looks, expressions, sounds and shifting
    movements.
Your Vibes…

Mokanla

Sistah...
Inside my eye cries
With only external dry eye
Knowing you seek my true essence
My flavor...my spice
Me being me, for you will just suffice
You honoring my spirit
my soul
my weaknesses and strengths
You blessing me
For without you
I could not be
I will not be
I would never be
The man I am for you
Yesterday, today, and tomorrow
Sistah...I cry
Knowing you lift me
Support me
Brought me to where I lie today
and where I stand tomorrow
In our world
No words to express my thanks to you
So I live in your honor
Honoring you in mental art
Of verbal thoughts and lyrical schemes
Honoring you as the strength

You breathe into the body of men
Honoring you...
Yes..... you
... ... Crying
Heart crying from the joy of you

Mejila

As dawn's rays fill a newborn sky
From the sleep, it starts closed to protect its tender shape
But as the dawn breaks its blossom does fly
Its color a sparkle of the sun's tone
Where are the roots leading to?
This delicately sculpted flower
So perfect the form and internally pure
Could its beauty be caught in first view
This image in my mind that grew
Bright red lip edges, highlight its appeal
Skin soft, smooth marble, perfume-smelling petals
Why has it possessed my mind so…

Metala

I've tasted many wines,
but none so rich as that April wine
Over years since that year I first found it
It has matured and developed a flavor that tapers my soul
Very intoxicating which has grown since the first taste
So I embrace the vintage for a longer stock,
a monopoly to the lock of its market
Such a lovely color and smooth flair
Like April showers it drenches my thoughts
Feeding it with enrichment and nutrients
Feeding my roots to come to life upon blessed air
Feeding my mind to greater abundance
and contain the insight of a seer
Drip by drip I crave endlessly,
as a wine-o seeking these essences to take hold
Bacchus couldn't have seasoned a finer wine
to drunken those that had no control
No control for the more classy spirit that dwells inside
    mentally
Too strong for the blind skeletons whose hearts are empty
Rare grapes not from the old country or the Silicon
    Valley
The location where I gather is sworn to secrecy
This spring wine on which I labor
My thirst for it causes my selfish behavior

More precious than a pearl that drives a country to war
 does favor
But favor the April Wine almost equal to Heaven's
 divine…
Glory.

Merìnla

A spirit told me to take it in slowly.
Take it in very, very slow.
The spirit warned not to take it in to quickly.
A slow inhale with no release.
It seemed so intense because I wanted it to continue
    flowing as fast as it came in.
And it kept pouring the way lava rivers do
A compassionate mixed laced from the base of the core
    product
Though the core took me away.
I needed this like so many times before
Because I had searched the alleys of my life yearning for
    it.
For never had I had a constant supply like this so close
I would usually fly high and far to reach it
But it was right here…
Close enough to not lose the rush after it tasted my lungs
It kept me burning inside to push the rush too
But every time is not your time… for you will be called
    upon when it is time
You will be called upon when it is time
And I felt the beats syncopate the rhythm of my heart
My veins stretched out vibrating the double bass tones
    thick, low within me
My total anatomy transitions for mental consumption
Until I was caught away
When I heard a siren say… Come to me…
Come to me…

Ever so strong her voice rang and sprang on to my soul
Was it my high… was it this lifting element that seeks thee
Unable to fight the song bleeding through to hear again…
Come to me
This muse had harmonized with my inner vibration…
not manipulating but sharing the voice mine had taken for a lifetime
She was that lifetime in me
A path that felt the extremes of the pain before within thee
And seek a joy so naturally employed to the world
Knowing I must vibe with her
Feeling the rebirth was soon to be and brought on a new theme I had yet to know
So I let my spirit go to her when called…
I let my spirit go to her when called…
I am still high but know I am letting go when called…
Called….
To her…

Touching Her

(Swahili)

Moja

Touch
Feeling
Mental glance
Deep warm comfort
Physical embrace
Voice resonates in the heart
Completeness of acceptance
Eyes penetrate the inner soul
Arms stretched out to soothe endless felt grief
Smiles, tears, joy, and fear, just knowing who cares
Touch

Mbili

I hear Miles singing to the soul.
These words that unfold
feeling the comfort of your words.
The comfort of your presence.
The comfort of you.
Feeling slow expressions of your ambiance.
Your glow of that inner to outer flows
That joy that unfolds
Yes, that joy…
Do you feel that joy?
The joy screaming out to you,
from those things that children do
That your children do
The joy from that one-second in time
Visions of scenic blessings
Perfect pictures of life
from before man was around
The joy to be mentally free
Empowerment of your personal strength
Seeing the world as what you desire it to be
The joy in each breath of life
Of life…
Your precious life
… Exhale with that joy feeling in your heart
So I may feel your joy in your smile
In your cheeks…
In your face…

The joy when the eyes embrace.
Sistah I desire to lift you up high
My sistah so strong, doesn't need me
But I lift you up
enhancing the core inside
Miles tells me of the dancing of your soul
Powerful, elegant, soft and smooth
The story so deep, passionate and bold
You are that queen that will rise.
Yes you will rise.
As you have risen in me.

Tatu

A line I write,

Our words do kiss and feel mental embrace

A prose I write,

Feel these words that gently caress your face
I wish to feel the passionate touch of your expression deep
These words that with your heart boils to race
Making memories of visions before our time to keep

Happiness

Each morn my eyes do burn to see
the words you give
the words you please
To reach out in your soulful bliss
Your warming soul, your happiness

Rose

Rain drops beading soft & still
A caress you feel
a velvet kiss.
Violet dark and deep
and richly defined
In this rose I may find
your name...

Nne

Concepts of ideals upon us
Not the norm, standard, average, conformed or
Assumed role within our daily exploits
A positive force or vibe of unusual, unique, different, rare
    perspective.
Never able to really pinpoint specifically or
Accurately understand the initiation of this feeling that
    inside soars
A cause & effect to curiously seek deeper & nearer
Though stepping with protective wise care
A chess game patiently awaits each move
Creating more options, neither good nor bad
But changing perceptions and desires
For each second the thoughts you have
When is the concept broken?
Maybe an open book
Then you have the freedom to search deep inside and look
But would that be too easy,
Taking away from the intrigued mind
Tell of the deepest feelings that have never left a heart
A part that is soft though sheltered, forbidden, but
    desiring for one to find
If one does search for the intriguing, please come with
    open eyes
And seek the core, to jointly explore the thoughts that
    you see rise.

Tano

In one second…
of looking into your soul
I desire to patiently
embrace your spirit
for a lifetime.
I know what your
iris is speaking
but I have convinced myself
to open my eyes
if I was asleep
and sleep if I was awake.
Wishing you were today's tomorrow,
while being trapped
in the pains of yesterday's tomorrow.
In this life
I breathe for God,
and share what is there.
In a full moon's shadow
you have taken my breath.
All this
as your spirit just walks…

Sita

Gaps are filled in time
of time's endless
spaces to wonder
Wonder how I
will be filled
or if I will be filled
with the wonders and
splendors of a joyful bliss
of a spiritual kiss
Kisses of fulfilling
aches to touch
and feel your waist
Reach the wind
of each skin hair,
can you feel me there
While I shape
each curve
shown in our interaction
of mind imagery that lets
our thoughts flow freely
Would you be touching me?
Could these gaps in time
show that mine
My thoughts are a lone
silent walkway
Or are you there to share
the lust and mental trust
Of the verbal twisting

internal bliss in joyfulness
Tell me,
or is this all a test
While these gaps
are closing in my mind
But thoughts of you
each second I find.

Saba

A soft gleam
twinkles in your eyes
After acknowledgment
of my silent whisper
Before your final goodbye
Feeling your smile
protect me from the cold windblasts
Like being fur encased
dreams of you I pray they last
Knowing that I touched your core,
It pleases me...
But as you do depart,
I will grow thirsty
Though remembering
what it was to be
Full from the essence
that I feel from thee.

Nane

I have you...
I have you in my soul
I have you in my spirit
I have you in my essence
I have you within the vapors that soak up the world's beauty
I have you...
I have you listening to the vibrato of my heart sing
I have you reading the Braille of my bloodstream's inner passion
I have you touching my voice... speaking as the wind whistling with adoring control
I have you in me
I have you...
I have you waiting to kiss my eyes
I have you waiting to feel the comfort of my embrace
I have you waiting, yearning, for each second of us to be
I have you waiting on me
I have you...
I have you for seconds upon minutes upon hours upon days upon moons
I have you through midnight moons wondering if you're watching the same moon with the same joy
I have you as you have had me
Spiritually blessing me eternally
Blessing me
So inside I cherish this blessing always knowing deeply that...
I have you

Tisà

Reflecting beauty and clear sight
Sparkling the brightest of sunlight pure,
strong and rich all the way through
A lifetime to last
Never turning or changing
Manipulating or rearranging
Symbol of the purity of a smile
The smile that is the catalyst of hope to inspire
Deeply inspire
Not too many can raise my mental state higher
I will always honor you as a treasure
If you were lost I would draw a map to you
You with that warm receptive face
To resurface as a special gift again
Intelligent and soft tender grace
A true lady in her space
She is the silver
Strong forever lasting
Pure throughout
Shining bright from the stars
In the heart internally lasting

Kumi

May the Lord bless you with comfort in your sleep,
feeling His embracing unconditional love rebuild the
    womb
as your cocoon to the safety of what the night avails.
Let Him bring your spirit to rise and stretch to the sky, as
    being reborn again.
As each day a mission anew, His tasks in your life grew.
Though He is there to carry you through it step by step.

As I think of your cocoon, your voice bathes me in lullaby
    tunes,
that brings endless rest, as my secret place knows its
    caress.
It seemed, I sensed I was so secure, each part of you I
    explore I would adore.
With my secrets too soon be revealed.
It has been so hard to let go,
a thickness, the Great Chinese Wall has never known,
feeling the presence of the Berlin Wall's last chip about to
    fall.

It seems from a lifetime we have known,
that our baby steps would show the foundation yet to lay,
    will be so grand.
A covenant communicated as strong as steel,
trust like a diamond too pure to steal,

but no expectations...
No expectations; only the Lord's guidance,
and our obedience will generate a mitosis in God's
 intimacies.
Intimacies of the spirit realm giving endlessly of ourselves
until we can feel the last drip of the blood pierced on the
 Lord's side.
Wow!

Knowing already that I will not be playing hide and go
 seek from you in me,
because it is a tragedy I never find myself that way.

I have lived on getting over.
I have lived resting on other's shoulders.
And for too long I have been begging on my knees
how can I be this man you want me to be
when I was either too young or too foolish to know
 better.
I can't believe writing this my eyes are getting wetter,
knowing I fight the trap that I decreed that bleed an
 endless bleed
trying to honor the man that died for me.
You have me freed.
I can purge to bring new seeds for your glory.

The initial catalyst that brought thunder,
this that you honored may part in wonder is understood
 why the foundation crumbled.

Forgiveness is not only spoken but felt, to leave the soul to
> let you float upon a universal breeze.
Internally expelled, not to tease each step on cliff edge to
> Neptune's end.

The power of my words are so great, since your embrace.
As my naked muse I place in your hands to comfort… me
…As you do sleep.

Kumi na moja

Early morn does find a whistling
I yearn you hear that whistling
Feel it softly breeze out my door
I hear your name just calling
For your voice adoring
Wind rustles in my face
I miss you more
Neglect to touch your whisper
Feeling nature's whisper
Whisper of your voice, so soft,
Inside it loaves

Kumi na mbili

Ever present is your touch…
Touching me, seeking me
Seeking my soul
I behold these vibrations around me
Essence from thee giving comfort
Comforting the surroundings where ever I be
My muse, soul mate, my drug like ecstasy
Touching my hands, in twilight's drift
Touching my mind, as a mental gift
Touching my face, skin, and inner passion
Leaving an imprint on my dreaming eyes
Seeing you with my every step
At every glance…
Not being there pours my internal cries
Knowing I cannot and will not be as one
Being two and as one
Being one…
With out you to complete me that my life will be done
Passing on to you now my spiritual rhythmic vapors
Vapors singing like Marcellus's saxophone whine
Vapors pour love essences of pure solute
Each day I dry up as I am with you
You are with I
Feeling that bond, that presence, that union that most
    inspire
Seeing your silhouette like a ghost
In the clouds, in the trees, in the grass

Pinching me…
In the stores, in the car, in my bed
Hearing the wind whisper your voice
My complete yearning desire to have you near
Living with your silhouette until the truth can set me free
oooaahh …
A tear falling…
waiting …
waiting endlessly …
Living only to love you
Dying to keep your love eternal…
Hear it in the rain…

Embracing Her
(Twi, Ashanti)

Baakó~

As I wake up with new eyes
Tears cry,
of the humbleness I should have of you
Sunrays glaze my face
For your spirit I embrace
So at this minute,
sincere & pure,
on my knees I now lay
For my sistah, in this I pray

Remembering my job to uplift you
Praise you as a queen,
is what I should do
Not defy you as an object,
as many brothas provide
Instead of seeking your inner spirit,
and the depth of your mind
With my brothas,
the Lord's laws they must seek to obey
For my sistah, in this I pray

To see us as one tribe,
the family
And view this, I see,
would blood bring harm to thee
My Lord had complete love for the church
This love we must learn,
to deeply within us search
We must touch you,
with the innocence of a child,
and bring no dismay
For my sistah, in this I pray

Your body is a temple within
To desecrate it, I sin,
a battle with the devil I cannot win
So I worship the ground on which you stand
I seek to a be a real man,
do what the Lord says I can
I want to just bring you joy each and everyday
For my sistah, in this I pray

Respect yourself,

so that I can respect you
Or these blessings I do,
won't reach or they will not get through
To be the victim of an ignorant man
Instead of joined in the future, God's plan
In these words I say
For my sistah, in this I pray

Yes my sistah,
my Lord let's me love thee
I can fail,
so I fall on bended knees,
then He can set me free
and be the spine of my brothas sincere
For this I declare,
not taking for granted why you are here
This is the prayer,
my heart now conveys,
to inspire in all ways
For my sistah, in this I pray

Mmienúm~

When I see your eyes
When I feel your eyes
When you pierce my eyes, you fill my soul
My joy flourishes as an atom's reaction to lose control
I feel heated fire like the sun's flare
You are my speechless wonder
atop of snow-capped mountains from 10,000 feet
Where I am in awe of your presence and glare

When I see your eyes
You become my sunrise never desiring to see my sunset
Wishing to be the jelly fish in your waters,
so I, transparent you see
Sharing thoughts so fluid like a waterfall within me
Seeing what colors of the day accent your cheeks as they
    smile
Reminding me of stories of the strong sistahs
that came from the region of the Nile

When I see your eyes
I see the determination like fire in your soul
Your heart is so focused,
in your life you're in full control
Your hunger to succeed does thrill me,
energizing my light of day

I am addicted to your mere presence,
you are a blessing to earth, God gave

When I see your eyes
It is not anything you do to woo me
Not a second thought in your eyes to subdue thee
It is just the realness of you being no other than yourself
Not have I seen a Nubian Queen with such natural wealth
In which I can pour as the river of the world as myself
Like a constellation,
a star to wish upon
brighter than anything else my eyes have felt.
So I melt when I see your eyes…
And inside I cry… joy
From just the blessing of knowing you,
growing through the vibe that you laid a petal
With gentle touch and clairvoyance that true.

Mmiensá ~

As you breathe…
I comfort you with touch as one
Touch as one like the sun against your skin…
Touch as the quilt that comforts your body with warmth
Touch as my words hold you at first touch,
Touch never wishing to let go

As you breathe…
I embrace your soul
Embracing your mind over seconds, minutes, hours,
and years since hearing my voice
Embracing your heart's need for the compassion I radiate
    to you
Embracing your spirit that has known me more than a
    thousand days

As you breathe…
I wait to know that I have touched you
Waiting while knowing you have reached me
Waiting while flying mentally free
Waiting… waiting…
I breathe you as your spirit in life embraces me.

Enná ~n

My sunrise is your sunset
Though your star we both see
A bright, lightened tunnel
Where our souls can be free
Forming like summer clouds
Our hearts twist and turn
Joining together
This passion now churns
A mental inspiration
A sweet song I hear
Each second you're with
In my mind you grow dear
I see your vision
Eyes are not blind
Viewing you across worlds
That most cannot find
I feel the Nile river
So deep in me runs
Filled with your essence
Glows inside like the sun
Future is unknown
So in your mind I now stay
I'll be there forever
At least this is what I pray

Enú~m

If you were not here
my eyes would scour the heavens looking for a reason to
    be.
Blur the vision in me before thee.
I have written of women,
ladies and queens across earth lands and the seas.
Painted words of their beauty, their spirit,
visions in their minds that I see.
How they touch me, embrace me,
brought me tears or laced to me internally.
These were my annuals thru time
that I had a need to have written down
Though none other has had such a profound effect on me

Without you I am staring into space from sleep.
Days with you transition to nights
with you never wishing to sleep
but live this day completely thru.
Days without you turn into nights
without you never wishing to fall asleep
without completing a night missing you.
Not wanting to sleep
until my last breath seeps out
and then my eyes would close for an eternity.

You see if you were here
I would lose myself in your eyes
as I have done a thousand times wishing to never end my
    life line
You sometimes not feeling
what I see deep in your existence
but you have let me explore outside of myself.
I have always been an abyss
channeling within my own energy
but not splitting as an atom
to spread the surge that I quickly dismiss
These thoughts that came to me since our minds kissed.

If you were not here
I would reflect on how your mind moved me
I never expected such a dueling personality
You have fed me mental jizism
that sparks theories on relativity
Relative as your glance that has me stunned
like a breathless mountain sky
The internal combustion of energy
for you makes me feel like I am high

If you were not here
I would edify you
like I was blind and feeling your presence would be clear.
Your scent well seasoned in my nose,
your lyrical voice of bird songs does echo in my ears.
I would feel your internal warmth vibrate against my skin
    hairs,

I would taste the wine of soul in the air… just like your
    lips.

If you were not here in the flesh…
Me would represent we
since we are in trinity
to be reborn each new day,
Giving all of our tomorrow
as if we both
were not
here.

Ensi~á

As I gasp my first breath you overflow my lungs
It was the early light that thru the windows caught my eye
The deep exhale that lets me know I didn't fall under the
 night sky
It was melodies that harmonized voices of the seven seas
Truly... Really...
It was your spirit waking me

Before day break clouds shift as ghosts
I see birds floating on the dawn of your spirit
that encompasses the range of my morning sight.
Morning breathes your colors into my light of day
Your beauty is beyond men
The eye of the pyramid is looking at you, bringing your
 spirit to light
You are the sun colored heavens that a camera cannot
 catch
and that only the naked heart can feel
If I look within the clouds beyond the naked eye.
I see her in majestic robes of the sun's name
Looking at the skies, the heavens are whispering your
 name
Her, that is that you, which speaks through me, giving of
 life completely
Gentle is your voice that charms my spirit
comforts lyrical harmonies to my internal being

The love of your spirit passionately grasps my heart
like beach water constantly beating.
You are the rain pouring on my non-fertile soil
soaking in each drip of your essence
You have bought buds growing internally
letting you decide to fertilize and harvest me
having Mother Nature comfort thee

I close my eyes and feel sun streams seek to wonder
if you were the shooting star that not so far rode my hopes
    on
I ride your streams for the dream of you
Knowing I would breathe this earth I would not die
Your spirit is one that emulates sunset glazed clouds
shifting to reshape beauty as life recycles into days
From the sun's blossom to the night's sky demise I breathe
    you
I remember breathing the clouds this day.
Your eyes twinkled their color.
It is your eyes I see when I breathe in the clouds this eve.

Ensó~ng

Early morn sky finds your ambiance breathe colors
As your sun reflections glide by my view.
I knew it was she,
She that would find quiet meadows and fruit trees
The fruit trees that my mummy would climb
Yearning for those sweet and sour tastes that would
    moisten her lips
Before she started up the tree's trunk
Not a fruit that hadn't touched her buds of flavor off her
    tongue
You knew her…
It was you that wrote beneath those trees…
Those fruit trees that she would climb
I see my mummy's stories bleed in your words
Like you and she share a plane…
Dimensional plane of adventurous wonder

In you, I see the warmth of summer flowers that I swim
    in,
Waist deep,
Spread on the horizon across hilly fields,
Flowers… the colors of clear spectrum bright of naranja
    to rojo.

In you, I wish to cry summer rain
That drenches my spirit with whispering joy

Joy that quietly echoes as the breeze
Whispering steady vibrations in my blood stream to my
    skin hairs
Closing my eyes
While hearing your whispering island song lullabies

In you, I want your image transparent
But pasted clearly on my inner eye
So when I look at the world
Your image would bring glory to each scenery,
Which came before my sight
Never absence from my view

In you, I see the spirit that walked island beach lands
Before a slave cried a master or a sir
Or is it just a blur that you are here now
Before songs of island freedom,
They spoke of she, that was of beauty, in the country
    lands
Rich deep green country lands, called da bush to some
She was molded by the country,
Mother Nature called her the island daughter, hija de isla
Island daughter that commands glory upon her Jamaican
    land
Her... home land

In the Gambia they called her Mansamusoo
River of royal blood that runs through her,

Makes her glow the way she does
She glows an infinite sunrise,
Only letting the sunset if I ever forgot her name
Her name forged from the creation of the four seasons
Seasons that start and never part
Until the next one wraps you into it's' world
Colors past creation's eye that fly free

In you, I desire to breathe your colors in me endlessly
The rainbow incense of my soul

Essence of Her
(Sotho)

Tee

Hmmm! Let me touch you in ways one has never possessed
Please just close your eyes and put your mind at rest
Feel the harmonic tones of my vocal vibes
Penetrate with insertion deep inside
Yes girl… deep I want to be
But not before I caress each curve,
And learn each ripple
Slow rub with compassionate massaging, molding, shifting
Feeling the beaded sweat, drip within
Kiss of the eyes sealed, pressing the exotic flavor
As we let ourselves go
Yes go…
Go and submerge into utter intertwining
Like thighs firm and hard and her soft as silk
Feel the warm friction burn the sensation to heat the blood
Blood rapidly flowing through the body
Flowing to the hormones exciting the minute, second, and moment
Of nails clawing backs
Of warm comfort
Of initial scream
Of the 10 second countdown to get up in there
Get up in there
Waiting, yearning, body begging to get
Up…

In…
There! Yeah…
Beaded sweat no longer now flowing molecules like slippery oils
Knowing you with more depth than any limb can go
Any hand, foot, arm, leg can go
Any part of me can go
As you share in me
Sharing in fathoms below the bottom floor
No deep-sea suit that can explore
Like you
You do feel me with complete and gentle exhilaration
Your easy forms of manipulation
Riding me internally
Riding me
Riding each slow wave and rolling thunder
To just get under
Under my skin
Bubbles under my skin feel like baby sparks
From the vibrations of shifting winds blowing over my nakedness
My naked mind…
Is what she finds
As we make a mental allurement explicitly
Not a physical grasp
Only the thought of our mental energy

Pêdi

I have felt a steady pour
since your bottle opened.
Slow drips
pouring mental submission
comfort my soul's existence.
One bottle shares
blends of flavors
that sparkle in my anatomic cells.
The more I taste
I yearn for a buzz,
short of a drunken spirit,
though a constant lace
of a mental and emotional high.
Feeling the vines of your muse
which are strong with destiny's grip,
growing carefully not to trip without fertilizing
cerebellum articulation
growing at slow cloud speed
with a fortress type foundation.
Wondering will this wine you drip
touch the lips of my mental harmony.
Island twist the Lord has blessed
being born into water
but filtered your spirit into royal vintage.
A flavor that tapers new life through veins…
I seek the divine essence just to move me…
Move my internal condition
to moisten my dried unseen soul.

Tharo

Can you make my essence drain through?
Can you make me drip my spirit into heated vapors to
    taper into your soul?
I mean can you be the ignition that sparks my blood
    boiling, rushing through my veins
Blood rushing and steaming my skin hairs
Steaming my emotional flares
Creaming my hormones fears to just be touched

Can you secrete my hormones?
Hormones burning from the yearning to feel the things
    that I have no words to explain
Make my hormones twist and manipulate my energy as
    water rushing upstream
Spin into fire, sting like a thousand bees
Trying to stop me from your ever-flowing honey

Can you transpose the water in my body as the full moon?
Creating the high and low tides of emotions pouring
Water in me pouring like sensuous falls of water heated
    from glaciers high in the sky
Can you harness the water in me as the energy?
Energy to encase you as the sunrays with their warm glow

Can you make me drip wet…
As the beaded heat blazing my glands to sweat
Sweat of Egyptian oils embraced by the pulsating texture
    of your skin
Drooling wet caresses seeking the mixture of potion to
    fulfill the soul

Can you make my fluid drain through?
Break down my composition into the ignition of a
    volcanic blast
Burning through you to start new life
Break down as a concentrated acid to make you high
Have you shaking, trembling, and yearning for that next
    fix
Almost having you to turn tricks for more of me.

Can you make my essence drain through?

Nnẽ

You are the constant drip to make me sip upon your spirit
Your spirit that drains through my veins, pumping your
    blood in me
Sipping on your blood with a vampire instinct
& letting you share in my immortality
as I let you lick on the slow drip of my spirit I bleed for
    you.
I bleed for you…
Blood taken from the soul of your fire
Fire heating your hormones that I sip to embrace your
    emotional vibe.
Hormones of what excites you,
frighten you,
pains you to cry or angers you.
I want to sip on each feeling that is bleeding through your
    endocrine system
reflecting how your expressions grow to embrace me.

You are the moon that brings the high and low tides
    within my flesh.
Giving constant waves of energy, pouring on me
    endlessly,
feeding me for an eternity
as your oceans find my foreign waters with exotic life.
The exotic life of my spirit that clouds a vapor that tapers
    spiral to comfort you.

My spirit desires to find within your mind
a capsule implanted to enclose my joy.
So each thought you feel,
my joy you will reel to each part of your senses.
Sensing me internally while my presence in absence
Though never absent in your walk of day
For even when you sense & miss me
I want to sip on your tears that gush like Niagara falling
Falling… in to the essence of we
I want to sip on the essence of we
Until my flesh is no more
Letting my soul eternally sip on the elements of you

Hlano

African queen
My sistah queen
I yearn my every days, hours & seconds to see you rise
See you rise mentally, spiritually & physically
My mocha, ebony, caramel, toffee, chocolate queen
Nothing but sweet flavors to the soul
Yes sweet flavors to my soul
That never grows old
Like a drug, I request…
Desiring more to attest my will for this addition of you
I appreciate the work of my sistahs
My, against all odds sistahs
My disrespected and raped sistahs
My single mother sistahs
My mentally suppressed sistahs
My battered, and cut up sistahs
Why can't we just love you?
Love the blessings that our Lord created you as
Love you as the soft breeze caressing the morning dew
On early fresh grass
Love you as deep as the volcano's core & the inner fire it
 pours
Love you as you,
and not to portray, taint, glamorize or defecate your
 image
But love that spirited, well rooted, strong willed,
 independent,

Elegant, cultured, passionately filled sistah
My sistah, oh yes, my sistah
My sistah,
...I love you

Tshela

My mind desires drunkenness to woe seconds passing like
    years
waiting to feel the pores of our faces embrace.
Moje srdce je tvoje...
desiring a destiny of endless thoughts
finding death to breathe your name.
If I never again look upon you,
I knew, that I once had been complete.
A blessing worth a hundred lifetimes found on this
    earth...
My eyes are wide
and my spirit is in tears
looking only for the joy of our union.
My mind now drinks to feel drunk
upon your essence...

Šupa

I am feening you...
So much I want to be high
I mean I am feeling the crack addict's empty twists and
 shakes
Yearning to almost sell myself for a...
Little...
Taste...
Of you!
I want to run through daytime city busy streets naked
 high
...on you
I need you laced in my veins
yearning a vibrating fire
making my starved hunger bite myself
seeking to taste...
the you...
in me.

I have to get you in me
Whether I can puff you in
Deep inhaling trapping you into my lungs
Vapors seeking each part of my internal space and having
 me buzzing on you

I want to shoot you up in me...

I want to shoot you up penetrating into the divine of my
 ever existence
Having me with dazed watering eyes
floating in the clouds of your spirit
while in day dreams of 70's halogen liquid colors

I seek the dust of you riding through my nose
Spiriting my cerebellum quickly
of powder lines on a path of your destiny
Possessing you constantly until I breathe…
no more…

I want to get so high on you
Not finding a dealer to sell anything as potent as you to
 dwell in my skeleton of bones
dancing from the songs of your voice
Voice allowing me to fly high enough to articulate clouds
and paint visions of mental sexuality
Sweat pouring as waterfalls
drowning in you again and again and again
between… life… and death.
I just want to stay high…
on you.
Until only our spirits are left
And we will float on…
past Heaven's end

Seswai

Thinking of you I exhale...
While pouring the essence of each thought of you
Into my glass bottle.
Crystal and sparkling glass bottle
Cut crystal like the diamonds of Africa
In this crystal bottle I treasure your essence
Desire your essence
connecting my glass pipe
I set the bottle aflame
Your essence transitioning to fumes
Fumes that now flood in my blood
Fumes that mold my soul
Fumes that in my heart take control
Fumes giving visions of the beauty you unfold
Your essence is the drug that completes me
Pours within your deepest fantasy
Sharing these thoughts that I now bleed
You and I are of the same creed
Please never lift me down off this high
This spacious feeling of having you deep inside
Feeling you in the inner tears in which I have cried
Watching the rain as I wait...
Awaiting that day
When my tropical rose is no longer just an essence to get
    high
But in the flesh to overdose instead
So I inhale...

Inhale the ever thought that spreads my cells
To give them the breath of life
Higher...

Senyane

Your natural hair roots reach deep in the stems of my
    nerves cells
stimulating the depth in which you are felt by my soul.
Your fingers whisper warm friction stories to every hair
    follicle on my skin.
Harmonizing with my bloodstream its rhythm.
Feeling my breath transcend and oxidize
synchronizing the sounds our lungs compressing.
Compressing as two from the alpha to the omega of
    existence.
Looking back on our existence
since you were that IBO queen who I was spiritually
    engaged to centuries ago.
We were the storytellers of our people
who filtered the rivers and rained glory on our
    communities.
You are the horizon that has no end
inspiring spirits from the oceans to the skies
as the blessed words you supply for world foundations.
The drips of your sweat
enrich the soil harvesting the new generation of Afrika.
Your soil was used in the clay
to heal my fragile broken composition.
Even the utterance of your name
puts me in a spiritual waterfall pouring naked on my
    condition.
Until I swim in your essence
transfusing my blood to bleed
as you.

Lesome

Why would I see past the image of skin on the palm of my
   hand
when my people have inspired a world and blessed this
   land?
I burst with the internal spirit that blew the breath of life
   in me
as I gaze upon her likeness
of caramel, cocoa, milk and deepest dark chocolate skin.
Essence so rich that make-up was made up of what we
   naturally possessed
…make-up was made up of what she naturally possessed
No suntan necessary to caress their skin, which they have
   been blessed with.
She is a woman that is deep in history
rising when unbearable pressure diminished the majority.
My sister's feet have trod the hot coals of the earth in
   their royal beauty.
I have traveled countries that stretch half of the globe
and the pages of my life unfold as I call them majesty.
I am in awe by each one I address
since they are not higher than the mountain.
Black women have raised white children,
cleaned the soil of the earth
and sacrificed themselves for scraps of change to give
   their family the proper nutrients.
I've been told that a black woman's spirit is too strong
   internally,

Though I feel necessary to fight the dual discrimination they see.
Reason enough that their persistence inspires me.
Like Curtis Mayfield's song breaking down his "Choice of Colors",
My ebony sister is the one I choose, my brother!
She has seen the ravines within my skin that bleed the history of our kin.
No need for detailed explanation of the daily battles we're facing,
She has shared the cries from my eyes
of the frustration of our people in the world's nations.
She is the one that catches my eyes on each of her curves,
not falsify her image of perfection,
Made of the Lord's blessing and not man's media puzzled prize.
The black woman will only have my eyes,
focused on her.
Her, that is my equal, my partner, fellow warrior and soul mate.
Since our souls have mated through life times.
Uplifting our life's chime
Of the bell ringing your song…
…in me.

Tears of Her
(Fulani)

Go'o

Is there, love anymore?
Not Godly, parental, or sibling love
But free expression of the heart, soul, or mind type of love
Following each other's souls to the ends of the earth we would take
Sharing one glass… two straws on a malt or milk shake
Matching our clothes with every chance in public display
Waiting for a kiss on the third date,
When we shared an entire day
Curled toes at play, submerged under the teasing crest of cool waves
While you softly caress me…
an infinite joy…
as a half moon upon us gaze
To find this in our decade, they're considered old-fashioned ways
The present lifestyles have studs, playas, pimps, & gigolos of today
Why should we be committed?
When sex is as casual as wine
Why should we be committed?
When in most houses, it's one parent that you find
Why should we be committed?
When we do for me, but were never taught the concept of "us"
I understand your vision,

After all those games, there is no one that you trust
A women of this decade is independent, defined, and real
Sex when she wants pleasure, to commit, her lifestyle she kills
A man of this decade, wants money, image, power, and to continue to be free
No emotional feelings desired;
Love is something he can't see
Is there any love out there?
Is that passion bug lost in the storm?
No love story at the movies,
Just shoot'em up, bloody fighting and quick sex is the norm
Is there any love out there?
A sacred vision quest is not seen
The touching, feeling, sharing, caring, switch your clothes wearing and God fearing,
Verbal less talking, hand in hand walking
Feeling my heart pounding; the inner glow is so astounding
Is there any love out there?
Who slept with you, and you were drunk too
Baby's daddy has no name, your AIDS partner you cannot claim
Lonely condition, what are you missing
Just walk in God's light
Love will come when the time is right
Do you still seek solo flight?
But with this question, I seek your insight
Is there, love anymore?

D'id'i

You are my comforter
Feeling your words, feeling your lips, feeling your voice
You are my comforter
Security of Linus's blanket from Snoopy... type security
Like spring time tulips, yellow, in a bed falling around
    me
Smells so gracious, floating on air so empty
You're the clouds that tenderly bring me down
Down so softly... gently...
You are my comforter
Just call on you
And your warmth keeps me from the cold
I's isn't cold no more... No more
I cry tears slowly thinking about your touch
Just holding me, squeezing me
Knowing the sadness I feel
Knowing the pain I feel
Knowing me
How?
God gave you the comfort
To comfort me
And blessing for my eyes to see the sunshine
That brought this dark soul to wake
Awaken...Yes awaken to a new day
As I learn again how to breathe
I seek purity in my heart
So I breathe you

So that I can live again as me
For I had died a many cat lives
Knowing self, but never, not one knowing me
So I breathe on thee
My comforter

Tati

Continuation of the ongoing daily flow stagnating in thought
I stop...
I stop to think of you
You bring thoughts
Like the breathing gust of wind past forest trees
Sunset drift watching waves move past the horizon
Thoughts like...
Snow top mountain fresh air takes my polluted breath
Feeling the passionate soft velvet petals so soft that you are
You are the light in my darkness
Darkness like that of no moon or stars to guide the paths of the spirits
Darkness which is the absence of light
No sparkle or shining item to keep hope bright
Until I feel you
Feel you enter my soul
As a new waterfall drenches me whole from your essence
You are my sun at prime
When the sun gives its most light during a lifetime
Yes, I stop...
I stop to think of you
You are the air that lets me start each moment anew

Nayi

Still feeling your presence, yet missing you
Missing the you that I love
Yes I love
I love you…
Love that you,
that loves me
For those feelings that made us free
Yes free
Free to build a true foundation
The ground that we stand upon
Was a new creation?
Mentally mind to mind
A deep chasm of intensity
The cross roads of our lives seem like destiny
The clouds of our emotions
Brought on a brand new storm
Rising from deep inside the heart
Knowing now that love can truly go on
The Lord's blessing for the spirit in us
The spirit that pours deep likes a rainforest's mist
Never understanding this feeling that came to me
Realizing it was a spiritual kiss
So yes, your heart I will truly miss
Pain I urge knowing when your departure will dismiss
My heart
Heart now pounding loud
From the cries of dry eyes inside

Drenching my soul
Feeling cold
But knowing
Our day…
yes our day
When I truly see the light in my way
Missing you
Will then be a memory?
While I spend our lives loving you

Joyi

Love didn't fall
on us completely
Because we didn't fulfill
us deeply in trinity
So without your spirit
I am forever empty
Since through
their eyes
externally we can't be...
...us

Jeegon

As I leave in my cold steps walking after the fifth hour of the day.
I drift quickly to envision the remembrance of the hours that preceded.
Your image sparkles like a constellation of stars designed in prints of you
Sparkles are those eyes like diamonds speaking to me stories of your heart.
Heart bleeding stories of love, joy, & remembering
Remembering her expressions, movements & habits.
Remembering her eyes, love & firm nature.
Remembering now for tomorrow's visions.
Remembering...
Remembering that she will always be there.
I feel your bleeding, the concern to share one joy,
One time, one love upon the shadows of a bloodline voice of authority
Wishing to relegate its self with thee.
I felt your eyes upon me softly touch
Since this night I was last,
A small joy from your multitude of transformed expressions
The night I give to you in open arms,
While succumbing to your soul the comfort of one
The passion of one, the stories of one
One who has known & seen you a thousand nights in dreams

With your vibe, my heart it does not scream
While feeling your face
This night I was yours fallen, tomorrow feeling your sorrow wallow
Feeling the following night of comfort I share in trinity, of thee completely
In this mirror of words that yet again desire to reach thee
In your crystal eyes that I feel upon the quick press of lips
Symbolizing the beginning of many moons upon moons
Remembering, feeling, blending the imagery of new paint upon a canvas
In your hands I give to you the trust to dictate us.
Feeling your eyes sparkle in my soul…

Laced to Her
(Fong)

Diē

Love her like the church he said
So if she is the church then she would give me reverence
 and respect
Attempt to achieve me as the center of her life and
would not forget my name just as the previous men that
 she had not forgiven.
Though I need her to drop off her burdens
Take up the dead weight she has carried within the earth
 and space
This way she could love me past the layers of dead skin
 barriers that she has used to protect herself
She would not need to protect herself
She could view spiritually, not allowing herself to depend
 on
all the weak physical relationship foundations that her
 heart wished she had forgot.
To open her arms wide with no fear of reprise
Crying her quiet tears goodbye washed through my hands

If I loved her as the church as this man
You see there is no deeper love since love is already
 unconditionally
Unless your actions deny my existence completely
Then in me, you would not freely see
I would need you to be free in me
Know that I would not take or forsake you
Use or abuse you physically or mentally

You should only fear God and not man's aggressive tendencies
Only tenderly embracing your spirit as music's baby…
whispering bird songs through the trees.
Being as steadfast and protecting as those trees.
Deep rooted in my path to guide you.
Be the support cast for your weaknesses and provide for you.

I want to love you as the church
To be in your presence spiritually never letting you feel lonely without me
Be the firm foundation on the rock in which you stand.
I want to be your world knowing that I am this imperfect man.
Rising, striving, inspiring to open my mind to find loving you past my lifetime's new morning.
Letting the dew from the dawn's green grass bathe and filter my thoughts to focus on she.
She that is the church of my existence laced internally.

Wè

Beauty as yours emulates emeralds sunsets
Holding your hand for our completeness
Resting your woes on my back to carry our load for life

Each day you surprise me with artistic features
Michelangelo priceless hairstyles, clothes in your unique profile
Showing me the facets and dimensions of your love

Your smile brings sunshine waterfalls
Heart touched me in the kisses your eyes poured
Feeling your presence in a glow being born from the fetal position over and over again

Your touch is as champagne bubbles tickle
As you comfort me with your warmth of lamb fur and embrace as silk rain
Listening to our breaths to syncopate and exhale in harmony

I am never without you, in my thought of day
You are the clothes holding me dearly, the beat in my heart that bleeds me

The fluid that moistens my soul to dwell with you
    completely

I want to cook for you until your mind is full
I wish to clean your house… internally so no baggage we
    can hide
Transparently building our foundation of yesterday's joy,
    tomorrow to explore,
and today we are the twin towers that can never fall

Anticipation is leaving your side at sunrise
Empty without you, but warmed by your voice in a
    midday call surprise
Rushing out a late day work meeting, sponging your joy
    when you see my face

Surprise is on a fellow's weekend
You come home to wellness and treating
Massaging toes to each muscle linked to your spine, facial
    treatment
A taste of wine
Hot towels to soothe your tension, temple rub to calm
    your mind

Unconditional confirmation is seeing the work and
    exhaust on your face
First cries then the Lord's glare on you as you embrace

What we created, the perfect confirmation that our baby
    in place
Breathing you and each day we lace

Destiny is seeing our children's children celebrate our
    union
Our love is the inspiration & model our seeds are using
Gray hairs represent the diamond we have found in each
    other
Mining each other until the sparkle is karetless

Àtòn

I could never tell you how much…
How much you mean to my spirit…
What started as hello, many years ago
You breathed life in me, gave me desire and set me free

We have whispered across oceans
And shared each other skies…
Dreamed of sunrises and sunsets
Though not at the same time

We can open up our souls
Like a waterfall into each other's hands
I have seen you from a distance
I have felt a flower's touch

You are the wind holding me firmly
As you whistled around the world
I could never tell how much…
How much you mean to my spirit

It seems like it started only seconds ago…

Ènè

I am listening
Vibration of your heart resonates to feel warmth
Opening your soul, searching, reaching, desiring
I know the story
The story you yearn to tell
Your thoughts I feel in your words
Words of passionate feelings
Feelings giving those ambitions and wishes
Do not look for a man
Let God fill you with wisdom
Let Him give you joy and companionship
Man...
True...
will fall on firm ground
Yes, I am listening
I understand the everyday struggle
That shackles your life
This generation of men
Are like the rivers filled with grams, and pounds of fool's
    gold
A shine that glimmers that is so impure
They are the result of generations
Playing the games for which they have already lost
Do not search for love!
Love God
When you know man like the ocean
Flowing all ways,

full of depth and meaning
Conforming to your needs
As you would conform in the water
Knowing your spirit, mind, & body
Once this flow of trinity is balanced
Love that is true will then fall like a shower
Let me know if I was listening
Are you listening too...

Àtóòn

Emptying my soul I bleed for you
Knowing that now is not our time
Is not our time
But look past the already committed man that you have found
Look to see if ever you could feel in me
Or is your heart for me empty
I am just laying a road to share your highway
Not looking today
But knowing that yes
Yes…I could complete you
Understand you
As I bleed my soul
For you to drain through
Every second you overtake my mind
Thoughts of you tingle all the time
To grasp you, feel you, I can see
To one day love you
Yes one day love you
Unconditionally
To be that air, wind and fire
To my Lord I declare higher
Only for what He is to bless
With this I confess, so I try to address
Touched shivering from your abilities on me
To truly know me, reach me, be one with me
To take away from this longing of feeling empty
Selfish not if you desired in me

These things that, to you I now free
Maybe you're just now understanding me
I guess then it would never be
And my discernment has been deceived
I thought I felt from you
What in a future could be conceived
I respect you completely, but with complete honesty
Your true feelings and thoughts are what I need
No worries about the pain I feel,
They would be suppressed but real
Always real but not destroying the friendship so early in
    its build
A lifetime I will lift you up
Whether you feel of me
Or inside me you do not desire to touch
To react negative to what you desire or say
Tears down me inside, as a man today
I pray with the realization of the truth
Joy soaring through me
Each time you are before me visually
Not dreams of ecstasy but of thee
Maybe you are only the dream that I see
My Isis, the Queen,
which I raise before me while on bended knees
But maybe I was right
Knowing I am waiting endlessly
Now in me, can you see?
Bleeding these words, draining my words,
Cold feeling I now have
As I bleed for you
Nothing left to do
But close my eyes…

Àyìzén

What is your flow?
Your expression desires to seek out love
The young smut adolescent thoughtless dream
That is the only thing thought of
Or is it a love type resistance like Montague & Capulet
Thinking you have found that one
That without them, death should be met
Is it love & hate you feel like the "Taming of the Shrew"?
Continuing to be mad at them, but without them you
    would be through
Is your love an instant camera?
Scenes of sunset beaches and slight breeze
Goose bumps drifting upon you
And the comfort of their touch brings ease
Is it that distant one-sided love?
Admiration of their presence brings desire felt
Watching their lips, face and contour
Makes your inner moistness get soaking wet
Is it the wild life extreme thing?
That drives your liquid fire
A death-defying leap of such
To make the love flow higher

Love...
Love... Love is
Love is understanding the true joy in one self for someone
    unconditionally

Love is endless...
Is this your love..?
Do you know love?
Is your love true?
Or is it falsified images to other's despair
This word to you, in which the meaning is not clear
Except its power to achieve selfish goals
And cause inner-formed icicles,
a devious affair
Will love ever truly be understood?
Seeking answers
With these questions
Love...

Tènwè

I want to promise myself to you forever.
I promise a word that is bonded to myself the ability to exist.
You see my words make my existence pure from their worth.
Following the ground I stand upon,
Morals from where I came from
Real enough to live right and not wrong
Not perfect, though God and I know where my heart belongs
So my word…
My promise is the imperfect seeking perfection type commitment I give my all to keep.
Wishing to share my life with you.
Share every dream, thought, and desire of who I am
While desiring you to fulfill each dream you ever thought about
From your first smile while your baby eyes were asleep
I need you to know that I can be me or sacrifice myself completely
So we will ride the wings past time.
Past my time… Forever
Forever is a deep spiritual theory which is past the fleshiness of my body
Meaning during the time we live past our last breath eternal into God's light.
Serving him while embracing your spirit with heavenly insight

Remembering our earth filled days
Loving our great-grandchildren as they run their fingers through our grays
Symbolizing the strong, rich platinum roots from us
In which our family has become.
From two souls the existence has become one.
This didn't start when the first child did come
Or did not begin when the "I do's" left the tongue.
It was born when your presence became their sun.
Though the sun does not shine each day
Sometimes not knowing when the rain clouds will go away.
When the wind's gust will rock and sway.
It is knowing that seasons will blend in time
while being as the sky letting dark clouds pass you by.
Letting the clouds of your life pass you by.
Forever is weathering storms through the seasons to season each other's flavor as one
Learning to grow together to the last breath from the time when you became their sun
Drifting as whistling winds forever
Promising forever our earth and heaven as one

Eyes Kiss

I yearn seeking it like a fix from a drug
For that sparkle and flash
The intense glow reaching to your internal soul
Moist touch in our visual display
To reach each other
Reach each other
Each other in joy, pain, and fear
Embracing without physical clasp
Sharing without fluid exchange
Sharing with no commitment or guilt to engage
Sharing a moment to remember in time
As I yearn for our eyes to kiss
Photographing you in my mind
Awaiting the second that you are missed
As…
My eyes… kiss…

273838